Kingdom Takeover

ANDREW OSAKWE

Unless otherwise indicated, all Scripture quotations in this volume are from the *New King James Version* of the Bible.

Kingdom Takeover
ISBN: 978-0-9858660-2-0

Copyright © 2013 *by*
Andrew Osakwe Ministries International (AOMI)
P.O. Box 8901 Wuse II
Abuja – Nigeria

First Edition
Third Printing 2024

Published *by*
Andrew Osakwe Ministries International (AOMI)
P.O. Box 8901 Wuse II
Abuja – Nigeria

Edited *by* Ijeoma Paul-Atiyota
Cover Re-Design *by* Adaeze Opara *and* Chibueze *Bibi* Kalu Uche
Interior Re-Design *by* Shagari Gwapna *(Shagx)*

All rights reserved under International Copyright Law. No part of this publication may be reproduced, stored in a retrieval system, or transmitted, in any form or by any means, electronic, mechanical, photocopying, recorded, or otherwise without the prior written permission of the publisher.

www.andrewosakweministries.org

DEDICATION

This book is dedicated to my lovely wife Ndidi, who is indeed a great woman of God; to my four lovely kids who are already primed to reign as kings in this life and to all the faithful saints out there who have committed to fighting the good fight, to conquering the kingdoms of this world and to expanding the kingdom of our Lord Jesus Christ on earth.

Acknowledgments

My appreciation goes to Ijeoma Paul-Atiyota, Oliver Dominic Iorkase and Salem Adum for their invaluable contribution to the successful completion of this book.

You will surely be partakers of all the fruits that result from this book, as it transforms lives around the world.

Table of Contents

Foreword 7

Introduction 9

Chapter 1 Thy Kingdom Come..............................11
   He Is Our Daddy 11
   Heaven On Earth 14

Chapter 2 The Kingdom Of God 17
   Kingdom..17
   Heaven 19

Chapter 3 The History Of Kingdoms 25
   God's Kingdom On Earth 26
   The Fall Of Man And The Loss Of The Kingdom..32

Chapter 4 The Kingdoms Of This World 37

Chapter 5 The Great Commission Redefined...........41
   All The World...42
   Gospel 42
   Signs 43
   All Authority 45
   Teach 46
   Make Disciples..48
   Nations...49
   The Great Commission 49

Chapter 6 His Kingdom Has Come 51
   We Have The Nature Of Christ................................53
   We Have The Spirit Of Christ 54
   We Have The Mind Of Christ 56

Chapter 7 Manifesting The Kingdom 59
   We Must Think Differently......................................60
   We Must Speak Differently......................................62
   We Must Act Differently 67

Chapter 8 Taking Over The Kingdoms Of This World 71
   The Greatest Revival, Restoration and Reformation......75
   The Mountains Of The Amorites.................................78

Foreword

I pray, as you read this powerful study of God's Kingdom, your mindset will be transformed. Your mindset will become the mind of Christ transforming this world into Kingdom of God. Now, do not be a hearer only, but a doer of God's Word. You have been called, appointed and anointed to bring God's Kingdom to your world. Our mission at the Wisdom Ministries Center is "don't just change your life... change your world." Now, with the knowledge from this powerful book, Go... yes, I said go and change your world! Bring His Kingdom, for that is your destiny!!

Dr. Nasir Siddiki
Wisdom Ministries Center, USA

Kingdom Takeover

Introduction

Jesus did not preach acceptance, tolerance or religion; neither did He preach human tradition or human philosophy. Throughout His three and a half year ministry, Jesus preached only one message, and it was a radical departure from what the religious rulers of His time preached. It was so outside the mainstream that it brought a great upheaval to the religious order that existed at that time, causing many to question their previous understanding of God and of the Holy Scriptures. It also threatened the authority of the Scribes, Pharisees, Sadducees, *et cetera*, because it was so simple and yet so powerful. His message was always and without fail confirmed by tremendous demonstrations of power resulting in tangible outcomes. No one could argue with the results that they saw Him produce on a daily basis.

His message was the gospel of the Kingdom, and His preaching and teaching were more than intelligent sermons. They were avenues into glorious heavenly experiences, which produced real encounters with an omnipotent King.

The word "gospel" is translated from a Greek word, which means "a good message", or we could say "good news". Jesus did not just preach good news; He preached a specific kind of good news; He preached the good news concerning the Kingdom of God. Yes, He was a great speaker, but His speeches were much more than rhetoric. His speeches were great not because of their appeal to the intellect, but because of their effect on the human spirit.

Jesus' words were so captivating to His audience because He introduced them to a new spectrum of possibilities, a higher way of thinking, and provided a doorway to a superior quality of life. The life and message of Christ were structured to serve His broader mission of mobilizing a generation that would advance His Kingdom and dominate the "kingdoms" of this world.

Jesus didn't come to impress the Jews with a new doctrine; He came to initiate the dynamism that is necessary for Kingdom Takeover, a takeover that has you and I as the primary tools of implementation, a divinely orchestrated strategy which includes the dispossessing and repossessing of stolen resources from Satan and which would then return us to the occupation of our original position in God's eternal plan.

The purpose of this book is to help you locate your place of relevance in God's Kingdom Takeover schedule and to enlighten you with regard to the realities of His broader, monumental and eternal plan for the church, the nations and the whole of creation. The following chapters will offer you practical steps designed to simplify your progress as you advance upon, engage and conquer this world's system with the wisdom and power of God.

Chapter One

Thy Kingdom Come

In this manner, therefore, pray: Our Father in heaven, Hallowed be Your name. Your kingdom come. Your will be done on earth as it is in heaven.

Matthew 6:9-10

Here we see Jesus teaching His disciples some vital lessons and principles on how to live victoriously here on earth. In Luke's account, we see that Jesus was actually answering their question, "Lord, teach us to pray" (*Luke 11:1*). The first lesson was concerning "our Daddy," that is, how to gain access to God on a whole new dimension at any time that we need to.

He Is Our Daddy

Jesus emphasized the importance of approaching God as our Father, rather than having to go through "ecclesiastical protocols." We do not have to verbally recite all the Hebraic covenant names of God before we can gain access to God. We can bypass all the protocols of religion and tradition and gain immediate access into God's throne room by understanding our status as sons of God and appealing to His fatherhood instincts.

When someone approaches God as His own child, as opposed to a servant, stranger, customer or official guest, nothing else has greater priority to Him. That person has found the tenderest part of God's heart and will receive immediate and undivided attention from the Creator of the universe. It is therefore important for us to have the right consciousness before we approach God in prayer, because though He is Elohim, the mighty Creator, Jehovah the God of Covenant, El-Shaddai the Almighty and multi-breasted One, He also happens to be our Father. The King is your Daddy!

> *When someone approaches God as His own child, as opposed to a servant, stranger, customer or official guest, nothing else has greater priority to Him.*

Just imagine that someone who happens to be a long lost friend of yours is sitting in the reception area of an executive presidential office waiting to see a very important dignitary who is reputed to be the greatest king of the greatest kingdom on earth. This friend of yours had to go through all kinds of protocols just to get into the waiting room, and now he is waiting in line with many others who also wish to see this king, but even at this point no one is guaranteed a meeting with the King. He will select those he will see on that day based on his royal discretion.

At this point you walk in and stop because you just saw your friend whom you haven't seen for many years. You are both excited to see each other and immediately start to catch up on old times and update on your present lives. Your friend, assuming that you are there to see the king in the same capacity as him, tells you why he has come to see the great king. To his amazement you say, "Oh, he's my dad." There is a pause and then he responds with a bewildered expression, "The K-King is your dad?" And you say, "Yes, as a matter of fact, I was just going to see daddy. Come with me. I will introduce you to Him." You then proceed to lead him toward the entrance to the king's office, and as you walk with him right through the entrance doors, all the guards and officials genuflect in reverence as they grant you access to see the king, who is your daddy!

Jesus was trying to introduce His disciples to a new level of access, a whole new dimension of relating with God. Through His redemptive work, Jesus would create a new way into the Holiest (where God's throne is) which would allow us to approach God with boldness as His children.

> *Therefore, brethren, having boldness to enter the Holiest by the blood of Jesus, by a new and living way which He consecrated for us, through the veil, that is, His flesh.*
>
> *Hebrews 10:19-20*

For you did not receive the spirit of bondage again to fear, but you received the Spirit of adoption by whom we cry out, "Abba, Father."

Romans 8:15

For you are all sons of God through faith in Christ Jesus.

Galatians 3:26

Through our faith in Jesus and His successful work of redemption, we have now been granted the privilege of this new, unrestricted, protocol-free access to the King of the universe, who is now also our Daddy.

Heaven On Earth

Your kingdom come. Your will be done on earth as it is in heaven.

Matthew 6:10

The next lesson that Jesus taught about prayer in this discourse will take us into the subject matter of this book and is one that reveals the Father's heart-desire for mankind and planet earth. We know it is the Father's desire because was Jesus' desire. Jesus' life, words and actions were simply a reflection of His Father's nature, ways and desires.

"Then they said to Him, "Where is Your Father?" Jesus answered, "You know neither Me nor My Father. If you had known Me, you would have known My Father also."

John 8:19

I and My Father are one.

John 10:30

Then Jesus answered and said to them, "Most assuredly, I say to you, the Son can do nothing of Himself, but what He sees the Father do; for whatever He does, the Son also does in like manner."

John 5:19

Furthermore, people's desires are usually revealed in the content of their prayer. It is easy to see in the sixth chapter of Matthew's gospel that Jesus' desire is for His Father's Kingdom to come on earth, so that His will implemented on earth, just like it is implemented in heaven. To understand the concept that Jesus presents here, we must first understand the concept of God's Kingdom and the concept of heaven.

Chapter Two

The Kingdom Of God

From that time Jesus began to preach and to say, "Repent, the kingdom of heaven is at hand."

Matthew 4:17

Kingdom

This word "Kingdom" is really a compound word which is made up of two words – KING and DOMAIN. A domain is the territory or realm over which a king reigns. The word "domain" carries the idea of dominion as an integral part of its definition. Dominion, as a noun means "supreme authority" and "governed territory". Dominion thus refers to the territory that is governed, as well as to the authority that is required to rule and govern over it.

The Kingdom of God can simply be defined as "Jehovah's domain", that is, the territory or realm in which Jehovah reigns over as King. In this territory or realm all dominion belongs ultimately to Him, even if He delegates certain aspects of it to whomsoever He chooses. For a territory or a realm to qualify as a part of God's Kingdom, three criteria must be met:

1. The King's word must be law, and it must be final.

2. The King's way of living (thinking, talking, and acting) must be the standard practice. The King's behavior must be the culture of that territory or realm.

3. The King's will must be supreme and viewed as superior to every other will. It must be totally observed and fully implemented.

Note that the word "King" here is a reference to Jehovah, that is, the Father of our Lord Jesus Christ who is now also our Heavenly Father.

> *The Kingdom of God can simply be defined as "Jehovah's domain", that is, the territory or realm in which Jehovah reigns over as King.*

Any kingdom on earth, above the earth or below the earth that does not meet these three criteria is not the Kingdom of our Heavenly Father. It is, therefore, a different kingdom ruled over by a different king.

Often in scriptures, especially in the New Testament texts, you will find the phrases "Kingdom of God" and "Kingdom of Heaven" used interchangeably. These mean the same in terms of quality but differ in terms of their dimensions; heaven is a vital part of the Kingdom of God, but the expanse of heaven is not equal to the full expanse of God's Kingdom. What I am trying to say is that the territory of God's Kingdom extends beyond the boundaries of the place called heaven. Heaven is a very important concept for us today because it provides a perfect prototype of what the Kingdom of God should look like.

Heaven

Heaven is not some esoteric, unreal figment of man's imagination. Heaven is a real place with a geographical location. Actually, it is my personal belief, based on the following scriptures, that heaven is an extraordinary planet that is located in the farthest north of the Universe.

He comes from the north as golden splendor, with God is awesome majesty.

Job 37:22

For you have said in your heart: 'I will ascend into heaven, I will exalt my throne above the stars of God; I will also sit on the mount of the congregation on the furthest sides of the north;

Isaiah 14:13

Heaven is the place where God's throne is situated. It is a place where our Lord Jesus, through God's supernatural working, is somehow able to dwell in and operate with a physical body alongside our heavenly Father and all the other spirit beings in heaven who do not have a physical body. We know from the words of Jesus, after His resurrection and glorification, that His glorified body is to some extent physical in nature.

> *Now as they said these things, Jesus Himself stood in the midst of them, and said to them, "Peace to you." But they were terrified and frightened, and supposed they had seen a spirit. And He said to them, "Why are you troubled? And why do doubts arise in your hearts? Behold My hands and My feet, that it is I Myself Handle Me and see, for a spirit does not have flesh and bones as you see I have." When He had said this, He showed them His hands and His feet. But while they still did not believe for joy, and marveled, He said to them, "Have you any food here?" So they gave Him a piece of a broiled fish and some honeycomb. And He took it and ate in their presence.*
>
> Luke 24:36-43

Notice that Jesus goes out of His way to convince His disciples that He is not a spirit. He eats some broiled fish and honeycomb and refers to Himself in this post-resurrected state as having flesh and bones. In John's rendering of this encounter, Jesus actually instructs Thomas to put his fingers into the print of the nails used to fasten him up on the cross and into the hole that was created in the side of His abdomen by the piercing of the soldier's spear (**John 19:34**). Jesus spent about forty days with His disciples in this resurrected, glorified body teaching about the Kingdom of God, at the end of which He ascended towards heaven right before their eyes, in that exact same physical body.

> *To whom He also presented Himself alive after His suffering by many infallible proofs, being seen by them during forty days and speaking of the things pertaining to the kingdom of God.... Now when He had spoken these things, while they watched, He was taken up, and a cloud received Him out of their sight. And while they looked steadfastly toward heaven as He went up, behold, two men stood by them in white apparel, who also said, "Men of Galilee, why do you stand gazing up into heaven? This same Jesus, who was taken up from you into heaven, will so come in like manner as you saw Him go into heaven."*
>
> Act 1:3,9-11

We should note also that at some time in the near future all the saints of God will live in heaven with their physical bodies after it has been glorified. This glorified body will be our present body in a glorified state. It will no longer be in a fallen state, but of the same nature and capability as that of Jesus; it will have both spiritual and physical qualities and abilities. Just like Jesus was able to transcend physical barriers and materialize in the midst of His disciples, through doors that were shut, our glorified bodies will be able to do likewise.

> *At some time in the near future all the saints of God will live in heaven with their physical bodies after it has been glorified.*

> *Then, the same day at evening, being the first day of the week, when the doors were shut where the disciples were assembled, for fear of the Jews, Jesus came and stood in the midst, and said to them, "Peace be with you."*
>
> John 20:19

For lack of a better expression, it will be a spiritual/physical body, which will no longer be natural but now supernatural. (***1 Corinthians 15:42,51-54; 1 Thessalonians 4:16; 1 John 3:2***).

So heaven is a place where the spiritual and the physical co-exist in a way that is beyond our present earth experience. The apostle Paul refers to believers as citizens of heaven (***Philippians 3:20-21***). If we are its citizens, then we must start seeing heaven as our "country." We must begin to see ourselves as citizens of heaven on an earthly assignment. We are heaven's ambassadors to earth (***2 Corinthians 5:20***).

Heaven is the only "country" presently in the universe where Jehovah's Kingdom is fully operational, where His will is fully implemented and His glory fully manifested. Heaven is the present headquarters of the Kingdom of God. When Jesus prayed in Matthew 6:10 *"Thy Kingdom come, thy will be done on earth as it is heaven,"* what He was essentially saying was, "Father, return Your Kingdom to earth. Extend Your dominion over the whole earth territory, so that on earth Your Kingdom will become fully operational, Your will fully implemented, and Your glory fully manifested just as it is in heaven" (my paraphrase).

The obvious ultimate result would be that earth starts to look like heaven. This was the original mandate given to the first Adam. This is why God did not create and place the first Adam in heaven, but rather on earth, and this was why God had to send the second Adam to earth, so He could rectify the errors of the first.

In the next chapter, we will go back in time to re-examine man's original assignment, to trace the history of God's Kingdom on earth and to gain a proper understanding of the purpose of Christ's coming.

> *Heaven is the only "country" presently in the universe where Jehovah's Kingdom is fully operational, where His will is fully implemented and His glory fully manifested.*

Kingdom Takeover

Chapter Three

The History of Kingdoms

Then the devil, taking Him up on a high mountain, showed Him all the kingdoms of the world in a moment of time. And the devil said to Him, "All this authority I will give You, and their glory; for this has been delivered to me, and I give it to whomever I wish. Therefore, if you will worship before me, all will be Yours." And Jesus answered and said to him, "Get behind Me, Satan! For it is written, 'You shall worship the LORD your God and Him only you shall serve.'"

Luke 4:5-8

Here we see an interesting encounter between Jesus and Satan in one of the temptations of Jesus. During this discourse, Satan makes very profound and audacious statements in which he offers Jesus the kingdoms of the world, their authority and glory. He then goes on to state that these kingdoms had been previously delivered to him, and that he had the prerogative to give them to whomever he wishes to.

Jesus' response was also shocking to me, and if I must admit, quite disappointing. Jesus did not denounce Satan's audacity or refute his claims or even contest his assertions. Jesus did refuse to worship Satan, but kept silent concerning all the other utterances, giving the impression that these were statements of fact. Could it really be that Satan was indeed making factual statements with regards to the kingdoms of the world and his authority over them? Could it really be that all this authority had actually been delivered to him? The answer to both questions is yes. To understand how this happened, we must go back to the book of Genesis and re-examine certain foundational facts concerning the original creation and the events that took place leading to the fall of man.

> *Jesus did refuse to worship Satan, but kept silent concerning all the other utterances, giving the impression that these were statements of fact.*

God's Kingdom On Earth

> *Then God said, "Let Us make man in Our image, according to Our likeness; let them have dominion over the fish of the sea, over the birds of the air, and over the cattle, over all the earth and over every creeping thing that creeps on the earth." So God created man in His own image; in the image of God He created him; male*

and female He created them. Then God blessed them, and God said to them, "Be fruitful and multiply; fill the earth subdue it; have dominion over the fish of the sea, over the birds of the air, and over every living thing that moves on the earth.

Genesis 1:26-28

The universe has over five hundred billion galaxies and is still expanding at the speed of light (186,000 miles per second). Each galaxy has an average of two to three million stars. Each star, just like our sun is surrounded by a ground of planets, creating a solar system. Of all the billions of planets in the universe, God who is the Creator and supreme King of the universe, in His infinite wisdom, decided to come down to earth and use it as the location for one of His greatest projects - the creation of a brand new kind of being called mankind. Unlike other previously created beings, mankind was unusual, in that they were made in the image and likeness of God, that is, in the image and likeness of the King of the universe.

The words "image" and "likeness" combined refer to appearance, nature, attributes, ability and behavior. To be made in the image and likeness of God means that the original creation was a king by his intrinsic nature.

> *God brought His Kingdom to earth and gave man the assignment of covering the entire earth with this Kingdom.*

The original creation or man was also given dominion over "all the earth," meaning that he was given the divine assignment of ruling and governing over the territory of earth.

The original man was a <u>king</u> and he was given <u>dominion</u> by God. When you combine these two words, you will get "Kingdom". God brought His Kingdom to earth and gave man the assignment of covering the entire earth with this Kingdom, by exercising dominion and by producing offspring who would fill the earth. Adam was to multiply through the process of reproducing this new kingly species, so that the earth would be full of kings who were according to the order of the Godhead, that is, in the image and likeness of God.

God's intention was to bring heaven's realities down earth, to extend His Kingdom from heaven down to earth. The earth project was a colonization project, in which the earth colony of God's Kingdom was to start looking like heaven. Remember that heaven is the prototype of God's Kingdom as revealed by the words of Jesus, *"Your will be done on earth as it is in heaven"* (**Matthew 6:10**).

Most people in our contemporary culture have no understanding of the concept of kingdoms except for those who grew up in any of the colonies (captured territories) of previous world empires or those who live in some of the present Arab kingdoms. These former colonies, having gained their independence from the British, French, Portuguese, *et cetera*, were made to look like the nations of their colonial masters in terms of culture and governance. The people dressed the same way, spoke the same language and were groomed to adopt the same lifestyles, ethics and mannerisms as their masters.

In these colonies, the word of the royal dignitaries who ruled in the empire's headquarters was law, their way of living and expectations set the cultural standards, and their will was supreme, superior and to be fully observed and implemented. These former colonies having gained their independence are no longer under the dominion of their previous colonial master, but still maintain some of the culture. For instance, in my country Nigeria, which was once a former colony of the British Empire, people still go to their places of work wearing suits and ties, irrespective of how hot the weather is. We still drink hot tea in a very tropical environment and speak the Queen's English as our official language. These and other lifestyles were adopted from the British Empire.

Another important point is that we referred to them as our colonial masters. This is because they were in authority over the colony. The colony was no longer our land because it had been captured and was dominated by a foreign kingdom; it was now officially their land. The glory of a kingdom is the expanse of its territory, so at several points in history you will find that there were scrambles between different kingdoms to gain more territory. This resulted in many conflicts and wars, and consequently

> *The glory of a kingdom is the expanse of its territory.*

there was much bloodshed and loss of human lives. Man was created by God to dominate; he has an intrinsic desire to extend and expand his sphere of influence and dominance. He was not created to dominate and oppress other people, but rather to dominate the forces of darkness that had been cast down to earth with Satan as a result of his rebellion.

> *And war broke out in heaven: Michael and his angels fought with the dragon; and the dragon and his angels fought, but they did not prevail, nor was a place found for them in heaven any longer. So the great dragon was cast out, that serpent of old, called the Devil and Satan, who deceives the whole world; he was cast to the earth, and his angels were cast out with him.*
>
> *Revelation 12:7-9*

> *How you are fallen from heaven, O Lucifer, son of the morning! How you are cut down to the ground, You who weakened the nations! For you have said in your heart: 'I will ascend into heaven, I will exalt my throne above the stars of God; I will also sit on the mount of the congregation on the farthest sides of the north; I will ascend above the heights of the clouds, I will be like the Most High.' Yet you shall be brought down to Sheol, to the lowest depths of the Pit. Those who see you will gaze at you, And consider you, saying: 'Is this the man who made the earth tremble, who shook kingdoms, who made the world as a wilderness, and destroyed its cities, who did not open the house of his prisoners?'*
>
> *Isaiah 14:12-17*

From the scripture above, you will notice that Lucifer (now Satan) used to have a throne which was below the clouds. If his throne was below the clouds, then it must have been in the earth realm. You will notice also that his throne gave him authority over certain nations, which he had weakened by his evil activities. This act of judgment and wrath resulted in a great cataclysmic event which brought about the destruction of the previous earth. This destroyed condition is confirmed by the words used in the second verse of the first chapter of the book of Genesis.

> *In the beginning God created the heavens and the earth. The earth was without form, and void; and darkness was on the face of the deep. And the Spirit of God was brooding over the face of the waters.*
>
> *Genesis 1:1-2*

The word "was" as highlighted above is a Hebrew word *Haaytaah*, which is better translated as "became". The first part of verse two literally reads, *"The earth became a worthless and indistinguishable ruin."*

The word "ruin" means complete collapse or destruction. We know from God's Word and His already established character that He cannot create something that is in a worthless, collapsed or destroyed state (***Ecclesiastes 3:11***). Obviously, something happened between verse one and two of the first chapter of Genesis that resulted in this terrible disaster.

I believe that Lucifer was the one that was given the initial assignment of extending God's Kingdom over all the earth; he rebelled against God at some point and began to undermine the nations that existed at that time. He decided to build his own kingdom with the resources that had God given him and in his conceited state went as far as attempting to overthrow Jehovah Himself. He became so perverted in his thinking that he actually contemplated an angelic *coup d'état* of the highest order in which he would usurp the authority and throne of the Most High. It was at this point that struck him down with such divine intensity that he fell back to earth with the speed of lightning.

And He said to them, "I saw Satan fall like lightning from heaven."

Luke 10:18

The Fall Of Man And The Loss Of The Kingdom

And God blessed them, and God said unto them, Be fruitful, and multiply, and replenish the earth, and subdue it: and have dominion over the fish of the sea and over the fowl of the air, and over every living thing that moveth upon the earth.

Genesis 1:28 (KJV)

When God was creating man after He reconstructed the earth, Satan and his fallen cohort were already present on the earth where they had been cast. The first instruction from God to man shows that He was getting Adam prepared for an inevitable conflict with the force of evil during this mission to re-colonize the earth. Pay attention to the phrase "replenish the earth" and the word "subdue". Replenishing suggests that the earth was previously filled up, got depleted and was to be filled up again. The word "subdue" is the Hebrew word *Kabash*, which literally means to conquer, subjugate, violate, and bring under control, into bondage. Such a term would be inappropriate if the subject being referred to was the land of the earth. No, the earth that is being subdued is not the land, but the inhabitants of the land.

Adam's commission to extend God's dominion over the earth involved forcefully bringing Satan and his cohorts under control and into bondage, that is Adam was to use his God-given authority to dominate and make them his slaves.

> *Adam's commission to extend God's dominion over the earth involved forcefully bringing Satan and his cohorts under control and into*

God chose a special area on the earth called Eden, where He planted a garden and established a heaven-like atmosphere and condition. He put the man in the garden "to tend and keep it" (**Genesis 2:15**). The word "keep" as it is translated in the New King James Bible version comes from a Hebrew word which literally means to guard and protect. This tells me that Satan was never supposed to have been in the garden in the first place. Adam's job description involved keeping Satan away from this special place.

It is interesting to note that Eden literally means "pleasure" and that some Hebrew scholars have explained this word to also mean "a spot of God's glory". It is obvious that Eden was the earthly extension of heaven, which Adam was expected to cultivate and use as the prototype of what the whole earth was to become.

Adam's first mistake, it seems, was in allowing Satan access into this garden. We know that Satan was in the garden because the tree of the knowledge of good and evil was in the garden and was in the vicinity of the encounter that led to the fall of man. Genesis Chapter 3 gives the account of man's disobedience to God and his consequent fall from his royal position. By submitting to Satan's will, Adam enslaved himself and the rest of mankind to Satan.

> *Adam's first mistake, it seems, was in allowing Satan access into this garden.*

> **Do you not know that to whom you present yourselves slaves to obey, you are that one's slaves whom you obey, whether of sin leading to death, or of obedience leading to righteousness?**
>
> **Romans 6:16**

Man, in essence, delivered his God-given authority over to Satan and, thus, lost the kingdom.

This is why Satan had the audacity to make the statements to Jesus in Luke 4:5-8. These were statements of fact. After the fall of man, Satan took over and began to once again exercise dominion over the earth realm, rebuild his own Kingdoms and run a system of operation that is a perversion, and in many cases, the exact opposite of how things operate in God's kingdom. These kingdoms that Satan built are referred to as the "kingdoms of this world" and the system that he established could be referred to as the "system of this world" or as is simply stated by John in his epistle, "the world" (***1 John 2:15-17***).

This system has been the driving force behind most of the world empires; it reached its zenith with the Babylonian empire, which is why it is also often referred to as the "Babylonian system".

Jesus did not contest the words of Satan in this instance. He did not need to. He had a much better plan which was already conceived from the foundation of the world (***Revelation 13:8***). This plan would result in Jesus forcefully, but legally, retrieving the lost authority, returning man back to his royal position and reestablishing the original kingdom expansion mandate.

Kingdom Takeover

Chapter Four

The Kingdoms Of This World

Then the devil, taking Him up on a high mountain, showed Him all the kingdoms of the world in a moment of time.

Luke 4:5

At the time in history that Satan made this statement there was really one World Empire in existence. This was the Roman Empire, which had succeeded the Greek Empire. There were of course many nations on earth just like the nation of Israel, but most of these nations were colonies of the Roman Empire. In the real sense and order of kingdoms, the Roman Empire was the only kingdom on the earth. All the other nations were under the authority of Rome, and it would not be wrong to say that the Roman Empire was the only government on earth. They decided how each nation would operate; they were the highest authority in each nation.

It is therefore clear to me that when Satan used the phrase "Kingdoms of the world" in the plural tense, he was not merely referencing the Roman empire or even the governments of different nations, he was by extension including every facet of human endeavor in which he had established his domain and which had been entrenched in his system.

Furthermore, whatever it was that Satan offered Jesus must have been something that Jesus wanted. If this was not the case, then we would not be able to refer to it as a temptation; it is not possible to tempt someone with something that they do not have a desire for. Some people have a problem believing that Jesus was actually tempted to commit sin. If you do not believe that Jesus was tempted then you do not believe certain parts of the bible (***Matthew 4:1; Hebrews 2:18***).

> *For we do not have a High Priest who cannot sympathize with our weaknesses, but was in all points tempted as we are, yet without sin.*
> *Hebrews 4:15*

I believe that the reason people find it difficult to imagine Jesus being tempted is because they have categorized temptation as a sin. Temptation, in and of itself, is not a sin. It is when we yield to a temptation that we end up sinning against God. Jesus was tempted on all points but refused to yield to the temptation, and so He was without sin.

I do not believe that Jesus was impressed by the dignity and power of an earthly throne, even if it was as prestigious as that of the Roman Empire. He already had a heavenly throne from which He had come and to which He would return. Jesus was also anointed by the Holy Spirit, which meant more power than any earthly throne could offer. So, it wasn't the allure of dignity and power that Jesus was interested in. He was after something else that was much more precious; He was after the lost souls that Satan had trapped and brought under his bondage. He was after mankind; He was after people.

The position of worldly status, prestige and power that Satan offered Him were tempting, not because of their vainglory, but because of the power of influence that accompanied them. Influence was the key, the subject matter and the allure. Influence was what Jesus needed to affect human lives so that He could persuade them to come through Him to the Father, receive freedom from satanic bondage and restoration to the former glory.

It wasn't the allure of dignity and power that Jesus was interested in. He was after something else that was much more precious; He was after the lost souls that Satan had trapped and brought under his bondage.

After the fall of man, world history shows that Satan adopted the intelligent strategy of establishing his kingdom, not just over nations, but also over any field of human endeavor that he knew would allow him to gain both national and generational influence over the masses of humanity. This went on for thousands of years such that he has been able to enshrine his evil philosophies in the inner fabric of these institutions.

These are "platforms of influence" or "mind molders" and have developed and evolved over time into powerful global institutions. These are a major part of what is referred to in scriptures as "the kingdoms of this world" and include the following: media, sports and entertainment, fashion, healthcare, politics and governments, law and order, business and industry, education, religion and philanthropy, research and technology, communications, military and defense, *et cetera*. With these, Satan has been able to greatly influence contemporary culture and then control, inspire and sway multitudes in line with his evil machinations.

Chapter Five

The Great Commission Redefined

And He said to them, "Go into all the world and preach the gospel to every creature. He who believes and is baptized will be saved; but he who does not believe will be condemned. And these signs will follow those who believe: In My name they will cast out demons; they will speak with new tongues; they will take up serpents; and if they drink anything deadly, it will by no means hurt them; they will lay hands on the sick, and they will recover."

Mark 16:15-18

And Jesus came and spoke to them, saying, "All authority has been given to Me in heaven and on earth. Go therefore and make disciples of all the nations, baptizing them in the name of the Father and of the Son and of the Holy Spirit, teaching them to observe all things that I have commanded you; and lo, I am with you always, even to the end of the age." Amen.

Matthew 28:18-20

These two scripture references will play a major role in our re-examination of what we refer to as the Great Commission. They contain certain key words and phrases that highlight the cardinal themes of this mandate.

All The World

The word "world" in this phrase is the Greek word *Kosmos*, and is the same word used in **1 John 2:16**, *"For all that is in the world—the lust of the flesh, the lust of the eyes, and the pride of life—is not of the Father but is of the world."* It literally means the order, constitution or system of this world. It is neither a reference to the earth as a physical land and water mass, nor to this age or period of human existence, but rather a reference to the systems through which Satan's kingdom operates on earth. It is a reference to Satan's government and so would include all the territories and fields of human endeavor in which Satan has set up his order or governing structure. "All the world" means all the systems or kingdoms of this world.

Gospel

We must remember that the gospel that Jesus preached and commissioned His disciples to preach was a specific one; it was the gospel of the Kingdom. They were, in essence, to go into all the kingdoms of this world and announce the arrival of a greater and superior Kingdom. They were to proclaim the gospel (good news) concerning the Kingdom of God, which is so power-packed that it is able to set the hearers free, save them from the bondage of Satan's evil system and translate them into a life of Kingdom realities.

> *For I am not ashamed of the gospel of Christ, for it is the power of God to salvation for everyone who believes, for the Jew first and also for the Greek.*
> *Romans 1:16*

Signs

A sign is a public notice that proves the reality or presence of something or someone. In this case (Mark 16), the signs would prove the reality and presence of the Kingdom of God. God has equipped us with the power to demonstrate the reality of His kingdom as we embark on the Great Commission. As these powerful realities are manifested and displayed, they act as signs to all people in all the systems of this world, proving that our preaching isn't mere words, but rather a proclamation of kingdom power and reality, backed up by evident demonstrations that confirm the authenticity of our words.

> *So then, after the Lord had spoken to them, He was received up into heaven, and sat down at the right hand of God. And they went out and preached everywhere, the Lord working with them and confirming the word through the accompanying signs. Amen.*
> *Mark 16:19-20*

Signs are to accompany the preaching of the gospel. They herald in a substantive way the arrival of a better, greater and superior Kingdom. They prove that the Lord Jesus Christ is alive and that He is walking alongside those who believe in Him.

> *God has equipped us with the power to demonstrate the reality of His Kingdom as we embark on the Great Commission.*

In Mark 16:17-18, what we see is not an exhaustive list of all the signs which are at our disposal, but just a little taste of an unlimited array of glorious possibilities. For instance, in the book of Acts, we find some signs which were not mentioned in the ministry of Jesus, like Peter's shadow and aprons from Paul's body healing the sick and eradicating demon spirits from the oppressed and possessed. Today many believers are witnessing signs, some of which do not have exact scriptural precedence. So long as these signs bear witness with our spirits, bring glory to Jesus Christ and do not violate the written Word, they should be accepted as kingdom signs.

Get ready because in these last days God is doing a new thing. He is moving in unprecedented dimensions and allowing us to have divine encounters with the glories of the age to come. All you have to do to become a partaker of these realities is believe in Him, believe in His Word and then step out on your beliefs. Start preaching and demonstrating the Kingdom of God. Kingdom signs will accompany you and your life will become a sign and a wonder.

It is your time to arise and shine! Arise from the slumbering inactive position and shine forth the glory of the risen Christ. It is time to stop playing 'church' and just be the Church. It is time to be who God has made you to be in Christ. God and creation are waiting on you to manifest His fullness on the earth in this hour.

> *Signs are to accompany the preaching of the gospel. They herald in a substantive way the arrival of a better, greater and superior Kingdom.*

All Authority
(*Matthew 28:19*)

The word "all" means "the whole of", "the greatest possible" and "every one of". "All" means that there is nothing left over or behind for anyone else. The Greek word that is translated "authority" here is the word *Exousia* and it literally means the following things: *power of rule or government, right, jurisdiction, capacity, delegated influence, and liberty.*

Jesus received all authority, that is, all the power of rule or government in heaven and on earth. Satan is simply a master of intimidation and deception. He wants us to believe that he is big, strong and powerful, and he has specialized in getting believers to use their own inherent power and authority against themselves. He then steps back and takes the credit.

The truth is that after Jesus received ALL authority in heaven and earth, He then turned around and delegated this same authority to all believers by saying, "Go ye therefore". All believers, so to say, have the authority of Jesus in their hands, that is, at their disposal. The believer's authority is not less in quality or capacity than the authority of Jesus. The believer's authority is the authority of Jesus; the authority of Jesus is the believer's authority. They are one and the same. Both the head and the body of Christ have the self-same authority.

> *All believers have been authorized by God to preach the gospel of the Kingdom, demonstrate the power of the Kingdom, subdue the power of Satan's kingdom and take over the kingdoms of this world.*

This means that all believers have been authorized by God to preach the gospel of the Kingdom, demonstrate the power of the Kingdom, subdue the power of Satan's kingdom and take over the kingdoms of this world.

Teach

(*Matthew 28:19*)

The Great Commission involves the preaching (proclamation) of the gospel, but it also must include the teaching of the keys, principles and culture of the Kingdom. Jesus spent

His three and one-half years of earthly ministry not just preaching the gospel, but also teaching about the way of life in the Kingdom.

> *And Jesus went about all Galilee, teaching in their synagogues, preaching the gospel of the kingdom, and healing all kinds of sickness and all kinds of disease among the people.*
> *Matthew 4:23*

It was a whole new approach to living, a whole new way of life. If people on earth, who are of this world are to be saved from this world's system and translated into the Kingdom of God, they must believe the gospel that is preached. When they get saved and become sons of God and citizens of heaven, they must be taught and instructed on how to live in the new Kingdom. They must now understand the Kingdom life and imbibe the Kingdom lifestyle.

To live and enjoy the life and benefits of God's Kingdom we must think Kingdom thoughts. To think Kingdom thoughts, we must hear Kingdom words. In other words, we must start hearing words that are different from what we previously listened to all our lives before we got saved. Kingdom citizens need to think differently in order to live differently.

> *And do not be conformed to this world, but be transformed by the renewing of your mind, that you may prove what is that good and acceptable and perfect will of God.*
> *Romans 12:2*

Our minds need to be renewed according to the image of Christ, and this is achieved primarily by teaching. This is why the early church in the book of Acts emulated Jesus by making teaching an integral part of their communication of the gospel.

> *Our minds need to be renewed according to the image of Christ, and this is achieved primarily by teaching.*

Preaching the kingdom of God and teaching the things which concern the Lord Jesus Christ with Christ with all confidence, no one forbidding him.

Acts 28:31

In the next chapter, we will deal with the importance of thinking differently.

Make Disciples

If we are not making disciples, then we are simply not fulfilling the Great Commission. Disciples are not just believers, they are believers who have renewed their minds and conditioned their lifestyle according to the culture of God's Kingdom. Disciples are kingdom-minded people who are willing and ready to be used by God in the great work of expanding His Kingdom all over the earth. Disciples are made, primarily, by teaching that is backed up by hands-on training and exemplary living.

Nations

When the Great Commission is carried out properly, it will have both national and international impact. This means that we must approach this mandate from a national and global perspective. Yes, we are to win souls for Christ on a local and individual one-on-one basis, but if we leave it at that level we will never be able to achieve national impact.

This is why taking over the kingdoms of this world is important for the body of Christ; the kingdoms of this world provide platforms of influence that give us the capacity to impact nations. "Nations" literally means *"a tribe or race of people of the same habit."* It is not a reference to geographical landmass, but to people groups who have integrated themselves into organized systems of living within the framework of ethnicity, geographical location or particular fields of human endeavor.

The kingdoms of this world provide platforms of influence that give us the capacity to impact nations.

The Great Commission

Putting all these cardinal themes together, we can now paraphrase the Great Commission as follows:

Go and take over all the kingdoms of this world, preach the gospel to everyone in these kingdoms, in every facet of

life and field of human endeavor. Demonstrate Kingdom reality, power and supremacy for all to see; teach nations to observe the standards, principles, culture and lifestyle of My Kingdom.

Chapter Six

His Kingdom Has Come

Your kingdom come. Your will be done on earth as it is in heaven.
                                                    Matthew 6:10

Jesus' heart cry and desire is revealed by His prayer in this verse of scripture, that is, for His Father's Kingdom to be brought back to earth, so that His will would be implemented on earth just like it is in heaven. For this to be top on Jesus' priority list meant that it was also His Father's top priority. The nature, words and actions of Jesus were an accurate reflection of His Father's nature and character (*John 14:9*).

In fact, this was the very purpose why Jesus came to earth. He came in as the second and last Adam to fix the problems caused by the first Adam. This would enable Him to return His Father's Kingdom back to earth.

Then Pilate entered the Praetorium again, called Jesus, and said to Him, "Are You the King of the Jews?"
                                                    John 18:33

Jesus answered, "My kingdom is not of this world. If My kingdom were of this world, My servants would fight, so that I should not be delivered to the Jews; but now My kingdom is not from here." Pilate therefore said to Him, "Are You a king then?" Jesus answered, "You say rightly that I am a king. For this cause I was born, and for this cause I have come into the world, that I should bear witness to the truth. Everyone who is of the truth hears My voice."
John 18:36-37

Pilate said to Him, Then You are a King? Jesus answered, You say it! [You speak correctly!] For I am a King. [Certainly I am a King!] This is why I was born, and for this I have come into the world, to bear witness to the Truth. Everyone who is of the Truth [who is a friend of the Truth, who belongs to the Truth] hears and listens to My voice.
John 18:37 (AMPC)

Jesus walked the earth during His three and one-half years of ministry as a carrier of His Father's Kingdom. The Kingdom of God was in Him, and He was an expert at manifesting the realities and powers of this Kingdom wherever He went. He was the epitome of Kingdom life. Whoever met Jesus had an opportunity to encounter the glories of the Kingdom and to catch a glimpse of heaven's essence.

Over two thousand years ago, God, through the life and ministry of the Man Jesus, started answering the prayer of Matthew 6:10. He intends to continue answering this prayer through the lives of men and women who have been recreated after the order of Jesus Christ, that is the born-again believers. The manifestation of this divine idea will be consummated at the second coming of Jesus during His millennial reign.

God wants to use the body of Christ to continue from where Jesus stopped at His ascension and to finish this job of covering the earth with the Kingdom of God.

Whoever met Jesus had an opportunity to encounter the glories of the Kingdom and to catch a glimpse of heaven's essence.

The body of Christ, that is, the church of our Lord Jesus Christ, is the only agency on earth today that has the legal and vital capacity to manifest the Kingdom of God on earth. As members of the body of Christ, we are best suited for this mandate for the following three reasons:

We Have The Nature Of Christ

When we were born again, we received a new nature; we received the very nature of God into our human spirits. It was at this point that old things (the old nature of sin) passed away and all things became new (***2 Corinthians 5:17***). We are now partakers of His divine nature (***2 Peter 1:4***) and there is no difference between the nature of our divinely recreated spirit and that of the resurrected Lord of Glory.

> *Because as He is, so are we in this world.*
> *1 John 4:17b*

This is an important fact because it explains how we, as a special breed of humans, have the capacity to house the Kingdom of God within us. This is why we are able to be carriers of God's Kingdom, just like Jesus was during His three and one-half years ministry on earth. Jesus himself prophesied of this reality in response to the questions from the religious community of that time.

> *Now when He was asked by the Pharisees when the kingdom of God would come, He answered them and said, "The kingdom of God does not come with observation; nor will they say, 'See here!' or 'See there!' For indeed, the kingdom of God is within you."*
> *Luke 17:20-21*

In other words, "The Kingdom of God will not come the way you are expecting it to come. It will come in the sense that it will be deposited on the inside of people."

We Have The Spirit Of Christ

The Spirit of Christ is the Holy Spirit, and He took up residence in our human spirits at the new birth.

> *But you are not in the flesh but in the Spirit, if indeed the Spirit of God dwells in you. Now if anyone does not have the Spirit of Christ, he is not His.*
> *Romans 8:9*

He was able to move into and abide in our human spirits only because our spirits were recreated at the time of the new birth according to the nature of Christ. Believers are now the only temples of the Holy Spirit on planet earth.

This means that the realities, the forces and the power of the Kingdom are already in existence inside the believer's spirit.

> *Do you not know that you are the temple of God and that the Spirit of God dwells in you?*
>
> *1 Corinthians 3:16*

This is a direct reference to our spirits and an indirect reference to our physical bodies. In other words, our physical bodies are temples of the Holy Spirit only because they house our spirits, which house the Holy Spirit.

> *The Spirit of truth, whom the world cannot receive, because it neither sees Him nor knows Him; but you know Him, for He dwells with you and will be in you.*
>
> *John 14:17*

When the Holy Spirit moved into our spirits, He did not come in empty handed; He brought with Him the essence of God's Kingdom.

> *For the Kingdom of God is not eating and drinking, but righteousness and peace and joy in the Holy Spirit.*
>
> *Romans 14:17*

Notice from this scripture that the essence of God's Kingdom is in the Holy Spirit. If the Kingdom of God is in the Holy Spirit and the Holy Spirit is in us, then the Kingdom of God is within us, thus fulfilling the prophetic words of Jesus in Luke 17:21.

This means that the realities, the forces and the power of the Kingdom are already in existence inside the believer's spirit. This is an awesome reality! It is actually our inheritance as children of God. It is a free gift from our Father to us.

Do not fear, little flock, for it is your Father's good pleasure to give you the kingdom.
Luke 12:32

It is unfortunate that this Kingdom, which has been deposited by God into our spirits, still lies dormant and unproductive in many believers. The truth is that God did not make such a great investment just so we could revel in that fact; He actually wants us to manifest on earth the realities of the Kingdom within us. He wants to answer the prayer of Matthew 6:10 through our lives.

We Have The Mind Of Christ

To manifest the Kingdom of God from the inside to the outside so that it starts to affect and dominate our environment, we must make sure that our mindset is in consonance with our spirit man. Our mind is the doorway between our spirits and our environment. It determines what goes into our spirits and what comes out of our spirit to affect our world.

Kingdom realities have to be allowed to flow out of our spirits if they are to be manifested on earth. Our minds can either block this flow or enhance it. It all depends on our way of thinking, that is, on what kind of thoughts we allow to dominate our minds.

If we allow Kingdom thoughts to dominate our minds, we will eventually start manifesting Kingdom realities; this is why the believer's first discipline should be the renewing of the mind.

> *Our mind is the doorway between our spirits and our environment. It determines what goes into our spirits and what comes out of our spirit to affect our world.*

And do not be conformed to this world, but be transformed by the renewing of your mind that you may prove what is that good and acceptable and perfect will of God.

Romans 12:2

Our lives are transformed according to Kingdom realities only as we renew our minds according to Kingdom realities. The word "transformed" in this verse is the Greek word *Metamorphoo*. It is where we get the English word "metamorphosis", and it literally means "to change into another form" or "to transfigure".

It refers to a significant change that starts on the inside

and ultimately shows up on the outside. It is the same word used to describe the transfiguration of Jesus in Mark 9:2. When we renew our minds by listening to Kingdom words, then we will be transfigured into Kingdom agents who have become channels for the outward flow and manifestation of Kingdom realities.

When we were saved, our minds received the capacity to think the thoughts of God, to actually think on the same frequency with God. Just like the mind of our physical bodies lies in our heads, the mind of the body of Christ lies in its Head – Jesus. We have received the ability to think on the same frequency as heaven. We now have the capacity to capture the thoughts of the Kingdom and think in line with its realities. We, as sons of God and members of the body of Christ, now have the mind of Christ; we can think exactly as Christ thinks.

> *For "who has known the mind of the LORD that he may instruct Him?" But we have the mind of Christ.*
>
> *1 Corinthians 2:16*

Chapter Seven

Manifesting The Kingdom

From that time Jesus began to preach and to say, "Repent, for the kingdom of heaven is at hand."
Matthew 4:17

Since we, as the body of Christ, have the legal and vital capacity to manifest God's Kingdom on earth, we must out of necessity learn its principles and develop ourselves in the skills that are required for us to manifest it. This is exactly what the Bible in Romans 8:19 refers to as "the manifestation of the sons of God." It shows us that the whole of creation (including earth and its inhabitants) is eagerly anticipating and waiting for the sons of God to start manifesting on earth the realities of the Kingdom and the glories of heaven.

The first step in the process of manifesting God's Kingdom on earth has to do with adjusting the way we think.

We Must Think Differently

The Greek word that is translated as "repent" in Matthew 4:17 is the word *Metanoeo*, and it literally means, "think differently". Jesus was referring to our way of thinking in this passage. He was making it clear that a new way of thinking was required for one to participate in God's Kingdom. This verse can be accurately paraphrased as "change your way of thinking because the government, royal power and rule of God has come." We are not just to think differently, we are to think in line with God's Kingdom. We are to adopt Kingdom thoughts so that we can live the Kingdom life. The word "repent" is a combination of two words, "re" which means "again" and "pent" which means "on top", or we could say "the highest place." It is from this root word "pent" that we get the word "penthouse."

We used to be on top before the fall of man. We were the representatives of God and His Kingdom on earth. We were given dominion and the highest authority on earth. We lost this lofty position when Adam submitted to Satan's instruction and we fell short of the glory that we were crowned with at the creation. Jesus came to earth to restore the Kingdom and put us back in our high and royal position. So He was, in essence, telling us that in order to get back on top where we belong, we will have to stop thinking according to the low patterns of a fallen state in a fallen

> *We are to adopt Kingdom thoughts so that we can live the Kingdom life.*

world and start thinking new thoughts according to the royal patterns of His Kingdom.

We are to start thinking according to Kingdom realities and culture so that we can operate from our Kingdom position and manifest the Kingdom on earth. Paul admonished the church in Colosse to think in this way.

> *If then you were raised with Christ, seek those things which are above, where Christ is, sitting at the right hand of God. Set your mind on things above, not on things on the earth. For you died, and your life is hidden with Christ in God.*
>
> *Colossians 3:1-3*

We are to stop thinking earthly thoughts and start thinking Kingdom thoughts. We are to think the high thoughts of God and no longer the low thoughts of this world and its systems. Once we start to think thoughts that are consistent with the Kingdom of God, then we are on the path to its manifestation. Thoughts are extremely powerful forces; in fact our whole lives will ultimately take the shape of our predominant thoughts.

We are to think the high thoughts of God and no longer the low thoughts of this world and its systems.

For as he thinks in his heart, so is he.
                                    Proverbs 23:7a

To the extent that we are able to think the thoughts of God, to the same extent we will be able to do the works of Christ and manifest His Kingdom.

We Must Speak Differently

The next step in the process of manifesting God's Kingdom on earth has to do with our speech. We must start speaking differently. Our words project the force of our thoughts into our environment and influence our circumstances in the direction that we are thinking. Thoughts without corresponding words are like a loaded gun that is never fired. The bullets in the gun would represent our thoughts, while the gun's trigger would represent our words, but until we pull the trigger our thoughts remain potentially powerful but vitally ineffective and inconclusive.

The truth is that if we think long enough about anything, we will eventually spontaneously start speaking it.

> *A good man out of the good treasure of his heart brings forth good; and an evil man out of the evil treasure of his heart brings forth evil. For out of the abundance of the heart his mouth speaks.*
>   *Luke 6:45*

It then follows that one way to help us get to the point of speaking in line with the Kingdom is to think abundantly on

Kingdom realities, such that our consciousness becomes saturated with them. Kingdom words must out of necessity be made to follow Kingdom thoughts. The outcome of every spiritual battle is decided on the frontier of words which were originated by thoughts. Winning a spiritual conflict is always on the basis of "winning" words that were spoken as a result of "winning" thoughts.

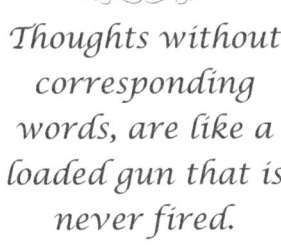

Thoughts without corresponding words, are like a loaded gun that is never fired.

The battle between David and Goliath was actually a spiritual battle, which was expressed in the physical arena of the valley of Elah.

The winner of this combat was decided before a single physical weapon was engaged. The winner was decided on the platform of thoughts and words. In reality, there were two important battles that were fought on that day, both of which were decided by thoughts and words. The first battle was between the armies of Israel and Goliath. This battle was won by Goliath simply because he was the only one doing all the speaking. He intimidated, paralyzed and brought great dread upon the armies of Israel, thus overcoming them psychologically with words. In this battle, no physical weapon of war needed to be engaged; the camp of Israel was already defeated in spite of the reality that they had all the forces of God's Kingdom backing them up.

And Saul and the men of Israel were gathered together,

> *and they encamped in the Valley of Elah, and drew up in battle array against the Philistines. The Philistines stood on a mountain on one side, and Israel stood on a mountain on the other side, with a valley between them. And a champion went out from the camp of the Philistines, named Goliath, from Gath, whose height was six cubits and a span.*
> 1 Samuel 17:2-4

> *And the Philistine said, "I defy the armies of Israel this day; give me a man, that we may fight together." When Saul and all Israel heard these words of the Philistine, they were dismayed and greatly afraid.*
> 1 Samuel 17:10-11

The second battle was between David and Goliath and it had a totally different outcome. In this case, David did not keep mute, but rather spoke faith words, which were based on Kingdom realities to rebuff Goliath's verbal onslaught.

> *Then he took his staff in his hand; and he chose for himself five smooth stones from the brook, and put them in a shepherd's bag, in a pouch which he had, and his sling was in his hand. And he drew near to the Philistine. So the Philistine came, and began drawing near to David, and the man who bore the shield went before him. And when the Philistine looked about and saw David, he disdained him; for he was only a youth, ruddy and good-looking. So the Philistine said to David, "Am I a dog, that you come to me with sticks?" And the Philistine cursed David by his gods. And the*

Philistine said to David, "Come to me, and I will give your flesh to the birds of the air and the beasts of the field!"

Then David said to the Philistine, "You come to me with a sword, with a spear, and with a javelin. But I come to you in the name of the Lord of hosts, the God of the armies of Israel, whom you have defied. This day the Lord will deliver you into my hand, and I will strike you and take your head from you. And this day I will give the carcasses of the camp of the Philistines to the birds of the air and the wild beasts of the earth, that all the earth may know that there is a God in Israel. Then all this assembly shall know that the Lord does not save with sword and spear; for the battle is the Lord's, and He will give you into our hands."

So it was, when the Philistine arose and came and drew near to meet David, that David hurried and ran toward the army to meet the Philistine. Then David put his hand in his bag and took out a stone; and he slung it and struck the Philistine in his forehead, so that the stone sank into his forehead, and he fell on his face to the earth. So David prevailed over the Philistine with a sling and a stone, and struck the Philistine and killed him. But there was no sword in the hand of David. Therefore David ran and stood over the Philistine, took his sword and drew it out of its sheath and killed him, and cut off his head with it.

> *And when the Philistines saw that their champion was dead, they fled. Now the men of Israel and Judah arose and shouted, and pursued the Philistines as far as the entrance of the valley and to the gates of Ekron. And the wounded of the Philistines fell along the road to Shaaraim, even as far as Gath and Ekron.*
>
> 1 Samuel 17:40-52

I am convinced that the precision and success of David's sling and stone were the direct result of the words that he spoke. It was his words that powered his sling and stone. It is vital that we learn to speak before we initiate any physical motion or action. Notice the sequence in the following scripture.

It is vital that we learn to speak before we initiate any physical motion or action.

> *He sent His word and healed them, and delivered them from their destructions.*
>
> Psalm 107:20

This, my friends, is a great principle; even God speaks before He operates, His word always precedes all His other actions.

It is obvious that David, while in the wilderness tending his father's sheep, had devoted most of his time to meditating on the realities of God and His Kingdom. His confidence at his time of conflict revealed the state of his mind. He had a victorious mindset based on his awareness of his covenant with God. His mindset was simply indomitable and his words carried the same unconquerable spirit. David did not waste his time regurgitating the facts of the situation. The facts were obvious — Goliath was much bigger and much more experienced than he was when it came to the conventional warfare of that time. Instead, David spoke the truth, knowing that truth is reality. He did not focus on the facts or dwell on the surrounding circumstances; he magnified the unseen realities, which he knew were greater than the natural facts. He understood the supremacy of spiritual kingdom realities over natural earthly and human facts.

When we speak in line with God's Kingdom, we are in essence speaking truth, which is the only universally authentic reality. You see, facts are subject to change but truth is absolute, permanent and unchangeable.

We Must Act Differently

Once we have lined up our thinking and our words with the realities and culture of God's Kingdom, then we are now in possession of the raw materials necessary for any other corresponding action that is needed. When our actions, that is, our daily activities and lifestyle match up to our Kingdom thoughts and words, we become unstoppable. It is at this point that we are in position for full manifestation. This is not complicated; all we have to do to ensure a Kingdom manifestation

When our actions, that is our, daily activities and lifestyle match up to our Kingdom thoughts and words, we become unstoppable.

is to act like the realities of the Kingdom, as revealed in the gospel of the Kingdom, are certain. When it comes to Kingdom realities, we must act like it so, because it is so!

> *And they were preaching the gospel there. And in Lystra a certain man without strength in his feet was sitting, a cripple from his mother's womb, who had never walked. This man heard Paul speaking. Paul, observing him intently and seeing that he had faith to be healed, said with a loud voice, "Stand up straight on your feet!" And he leaped and walked.*
>
> *Acts 14:7-10*

As Paul was preaching the gospel of the Kingdom in Lystra, this man who had a congenital deformity was listening to his message with rapt attention. As he listened to the power-packed gospel that Paul preached, it must have seriously affected his thought process. In spite of the fact that he was born a cripple, he started to see himself in the light of Kingdom realities. He saw himself whole and healthy. He saw himself walking normally and living an ailment-free life. As we examine this event, let us not forget one of the pivotal concepts of the gospel which we previously looked at in Matthew 6:10.

> *Your kingdom come. Your will be done on earth as it is in heaven.*
>
> *Matthew 6:10*

As Paul preached in Lystra, this man must have come to the realization that there is no sickness or deformity in heaven. Based on this picture, he could see that his present unfortunate condition was not consistent with Kingdom realities. However, without taking any corresponding action, he still remained in his crippled condition. This man must have experienced an inner conflict, struggling in his thoughts between the realities that were painted through the words of the Apostle Paul and the obvious facts of his condition. He had the faith to be healed and made whole, but he was still deformed! This interesting mixture of faith and uncertainty concerning the next step to take was expressed by his body language and is probably what Paul observed.

> *This man heard Paul speaking. Paul, observing him intently and seeing that he had faith to be healed.*
> *Acts 14:9*

Paul knew something that this man did not know. Paul knew the missing piece of the information puzzle, which is that the only factor that stands between a faith-filled person and their manifestation is their corresponding action of faith.

> *Thus also faith by itself, if it does not have works, is dead.*
> *James 2:17*

> *For as the body without the spirit is dead, so faith without works is dead also.*
> *James 2:26*

Paul issued an instruction to the crippled man, which was intended to provoke an action that corresponded to the man's faith. The man responded appropriately and by so doing he stepped into his manifestation. The Kingdom of God was manifested that day in Lystra, in plain sight of everyone, causing them to testify of the supernatural power of the gospel.

> *Now when the people saw what Paul had done, they raised their voices, saying in the Lycaonian language, "The gods have come down to us in the likeness of men!"*
>
> *Acts 14:11*

Chapter Eight

Taking Over The Kingdoms Of This World

> *Then the seventh angel sounded: And there were loud voices in heaven, saying, "The kingdoms of this world have become the kingdoms of our Lord and of His Christ, and He shall reign forever and ever."*
>
> *Revelation 11:15*

The above verse tells us *"the kingdoms of this world have become"*. Notice that they are not about to become, but have already become, as a past tense reality. The question is, at what point did these kingdoms become the Kingdom of our Lord and His Christ? The answer is simple; when Jesus, through His redemptive death, went into the enclaves of hell. He not only rescued

> *He not only rescued mankind from Satan's binding clench and control, but He also dethroned Satan from the place of authority.*

mankind from Satan's binding clench and control, but He also dethroned Satan from the place of authority, which he had deceptively taken from man in the Garden of Eden.

> *[God] disarmed the principalities and powers that were ranged against us and made a bold display and public example of them, in triumphing over them in Him and in it [the cross].*
>
> *Colossians 2:15 (AMPC)*

> *He has delivered us from the power of darkness and conveyed us into the kingdom of the Son of His love, in whom we have redemption through His blood, the forgiveness of sins.*
>
> *Colossians 1:13-14*

> *We do discuss 'wisdom' with those who are mature; only it is not the wisdom of this world or of the dethroned Powers who rule this world.*
>
> *1 Corinthians 2:6 (MOFFATS)*

Whatever belongs to Jesus by inheritance or by conquest also belongs to the Church, by reason of our union with Him.

Through His work of redemption, Jesus was able to forcefully but legally retrieve man's lost authority, return man back to his royal position and reestablish the original Kingdom expansion mandate, as we saw earlier.

So, legally speaking, the kingdoms of this world have become the property "of our Lord and of His Christ."

The phrase "His Christ" is a reference to the corporate spiritual entity, which has Jesus as its head and the church as its body. Whatever belongs to Jesus by inheritance or by conquest also belongs to the Church, by reason of our union with Him.

> *But he who is joined to the Lord is one spirit with Him.*
> *1 Corinthians 6:17*

> *The Spirit Himself bears witness with our spirit that we are children of God, and if children, then heirs— heirs of God and joint heirs with Christ, if indeed we suffer with Him, that we may also be glorified together.*
> *Romans 8:16-17*

The kingdoms of this world now belong to Jesus Christ by conquest and by inheritance. They also belong to the church, that is, all the children of God, being joint heirs with Christ. The phrase "joint heirs" does not mean part ownership; it means joint ownership. It is not a fifty-fifty deal, but a hundred percent deal, in which we own whatever He owns, and He owns whatever we own.

Like we have already seen, the truth of the matter is that even though the kingdoms of the world now belong to the Church, they are still to a large extent in the possession of Satan and his forces. For about two thousand years the Church has played religion, being content with dead ritualistic activities, while Satan has systematically strengthened his presence in these kingdoms, using them as platforms to influence and destroy masses of humanity over several generations. The church at some point in history seemed to have lost its focus and ended up building denominations, instead of manifesting God's glory and taking over the kingdoms which it was mandated to possess.

Our assignment, the Great Commission, is to advance forcefully by the power and wisdom of God as the primary agents of His mighty Kingdom on earth and then take over all the kingdoms in this world. We already have the legal authority and the right of ownership over these kingdoms, so all we are expected to do is to dispossess these kingdoms from Satan and repossess them for God, bringing them back under the auspices of His Kingdom. We are on a "dispossession and repossession mission," and the abundant grace of Jesus Christ has been made available for us to get the job done.

> *And in the days of these kings the God of heaven will set up a kingdom which shall never be destroyed; and the kingdom shall not be left to other people; it shall break in pieces and consume all these kingdoms, and it shall stand forever. Inasmuch as you saw that the stone was cut out of the mountain without hands, and that it broke in pieces the iron, the bronze, the clay, the silver, and the gold—the great God has made known to the king what will come to pass after this. The dream is certain, and its interpretation is sure.*
>
> Daniel 2:44-45

These verses in the second chapter of the book of Daniel record the interpretation that God gave to Daniel concerning King Nebuchadnezzar's dream. In this interpretation we see that several kingdoms would rise over time, but a Kingdom of a different nature and order set up by God would overcome and consume all these other kingdoms. This Kingdom of God is symbolized as the stone which was cut out of the mountain without hands.

> *Now it shall come to pass in the latter days that the mountain of the Lord's house shall be established on the top of the mountains, and shall be exalted above the hills; and peoples shall flow to it.*
> *Micah 4:1*

The word "mountain" is often used in scripture to symbolize kingdoms, especially when it is not given a specific name, or used within the context of a specific geographical location, as in the case above. Here, the prophet Micah gives a prophecy concerning the last days (latter days). He shows by the Spirit that in the last days the Kingdom of God would be established on top of all other kingdoms, that is, it will gain supremacy over the rest. This would result in a great influx of people into the Kingdom; multitudes will be saved as a result of the Church of Christ taking over the kingdoms in this world.

The Greatest Revival, Restoration And Reformation

Many of God's authentic prophets have prophesied about the greatest revival in the history of humanity that is about to take place sometime around the early part of this twenty-first century. This revival is imminent! God is already at work,

> *God is already at work, setting the stage by repositioning His people for a great Kingdom takeover.*

setting the stage by repositioning His people for a great Kingdom takeover.

This great Kingdom takeover will precede the great revival that we have been waiting for. Previous revivals have been, to a large extent, wasted because they were not properly translated into kingdom advancement or channeled effectively towards producing restoration in the body of Christ and cultural reformation on a national and international scale.

We must never forget that the "Great Commission" is a divine mandate designed to effect national reformation. Our discipling should result in nations becoming dwelling places for God's glory, looking and operating like the Kingdom of God.

> **Go therefore and make disciples of all the nations, baptizing them in the name of the Father and of the Son and of the Holy Spirit, teaching them to observe all things that I have commanded you; and lo, I am with you always, even to the end of the age. Amen.**
>
> *Matthew 28:19-20*

In the millennium, the nations, which are reformed as such, will be referred to as "sheep nations" while the rest will be referred to as "goat nations." At the judgment of nations, the sheep nations will inherit the fullness of the Kingdom on earth, while the goat nations will be destroyed with Satan. (*Matthew 25:31-34,41*)

You see, my friends, it is vitally important that the greatest revival takes place not just in our church auditoriums, but even more so in all the kingdoms of this world. We must take the revival power of God into the arenas of media, sports and entertainment, fashion, healthcare, politics and governments, law and order, business and industry, education, religion and philanthropy, research and technology, communications, military and defense, and whichever field of human endeavor that we have been called to.

> *We must never forget that the "Great Commission" is a divine mandate designed to effect national reformation.*

This is the only way to guarantee that the greatest restoration, reformation and influx of souls into the Kingdom is achieved according to God's plan for the last days. We must take the glory of God and His Kingdom outside the walls of the church and into the highways, byways, marketplace, and into every conceivable field of human endeavor. Then we must take over these Kingdoms and influence our generation for Christ by taking advantage of the platforms that they provide.

The Mountains Of The Amorites

The Lord our God spoke to us in Horeb, saying: 'You have dwelt long enough at this mountain. Turn and take your journey, and go to the mountains of the Amorites, to all the neighboring places in the plain, in the mountains and in the lowland, in the South and on the seacoast, to the land of the Canaanites and to Lebanon, as far as the great river, the River Euphrates.'

Deuteronomy 1:6-7

The possession of the Promised Land by the children of Israel was a picture and shadow of the actual possession of God's promised inheritance by the church in the New Covenant. *"The mountains of the Amorites"* are types of the kingdoms of this world. The entrance into and possession of the Promised Land at the time of the Old Covenant is a picture of the future New Covenant restoration of the Kingdom, the power, and the glory, which Adam lost in the garden. It is also a picture of the advancement and forceful possession of all the kingdoms in this world by the Church in the last days.

Just as in the case with Israel in Mount Horeb, today God is telling the body of Christ that we have dwelt long enough "at this mountain". That is, we have lost our proper focus, with the result that we have wasted years wandering around in circles within the confines of the "church world" as opposed to going into the "outside world" and taking over the kingdoms in it. We have become comfortable in our beautiful churches, experiencing great moves of the Spirit, but remaining in the same status and position year after year, while the world immediately outside our church doors continues to die and go to hell.

> *Woe to you who are at ease in Zion, and trust in Mount Samaria.*
> *Amos 6:1a*

This is one reason why the church is experiencing so much infighting, strife, divisions and splits. If most believers were busy strategizing on how to take over kingdoms and actually applying their spiritual might against Satan's forces by fighting the good fight and taking over the kingdoms in this world, they would not have the time or the desire to backbite, bicker and fight with each other.

Most of these believers do not know what to do with all the authority and power that now resides on their insides. They are fighting, but it is the wrong fight. It is in the wrong venue, so it keeps leading to frustration, self-defeat and self-destruction, thus hindering many of the great Kingdom projects that are meant to produce significant global impact. Brethren, we have dwelt long enough at the mountain of religious complacency. Let us turn, take our journey, and go take over the "mountains of the Amorites."

May the message of this book trigger in you a greater hunger to fulfil the Great Commission and help you run a much more focused race than you have in past times. May God strengthen you, by His grace, to confront and engage the world's system and overcome it, so that the Kingdom of God

> *Brethren, we have dwelt long enough at the mountain of religious complacency. Let us turn, take our journey, and go take over the "mountains of the Amorites."*

will take its rightful place on earth and draw multitudes to Christ.

We must not allow fear and discouragement to stop our forceful advancement. God is not just with us; He now lives and abides in us. We have become carriers of deity, and so there is no room for defeat. Your time to take your pre-ordained position and shine forth your light has come! Your time to arise in the full splendor of God's glory, tap into His abundant grace and take over the kingdoms that you have been called into has come! Go in this might of yours and do not look back. Amen!

> *And I said to you, 'You have come to the mountains of the Amorites, which the LORD our God is giving us. Look, the LORD your God has set the land before you; go up and possess it, as the LORD God of your fathers has spoken to you; do not fear or be discouraged.'*
>
> *Deuteronomy 1:20-21*
>
> *And I commanded Joshua at that time, saying, 'Your eyes have seen all that the LORD your God has done to these two kings; so will the LORD do to all the*

kingdoms through which you pass. You must not fear them, for the LORD your God Himself fights for you.'

Deuteronomy 3:20-22

Kingdom Takeover

Other BOOKS *by* ANDREW OSAKWE

Running With A Vision
This timely book will show you how to cooperate with God as you strive to do His will and realize your full potential in life. It is laden with fresh insight on the power, process and priceless steps required to accomplish great visions.

The Mission Is Possible
This book will help you identify your life's mission, teach you to access God's blueprint for your life, equip you with the practical steps that will guarantee true success, show you how to enjoy the journey on your way to your place of fullness and empower you to overcome all obstacles.

Ethics of Ministry and Christian Living
The principles shared in this book will help to clear the way for the greatest kingdom expansion movement that has ever been witnessed on earth. You will learn the relevant principles of ministerial ethics especially as it applies to our modern culture.

Entrepreneurial Leadership
God is raising "leading entrepreneurs" through whom He will raise the standards, sanitize the industries and provide the necessary spiritual guidance that is needed in the market spaces. In this book, you will learn how to chart the path for new ideas and discover new ways of doing business that will lead you back to the truth and bring glory to God.

Hermeneutics: Simple Keys to Bible Study and Interpretation
Wrong Bible interpretation is the reason for a lot of the errors and confusion that we find today concerning the scriptures. It has also created the erroneous impression that the Bible is difficult to understand and that it is not possible to find consistency in interpretation. The reality, however, is that the Bible is actually quite easy to understand. The purpose of this book is to present you with a non-complicated way of reading and studying your Bible by explaining in a simple, easy to understand way the most effective methods of interpretation.

POWER CONFESSIONS: 40 Days of Glorious Meditation
Being prosperous and having good success are the results of constant meditation on the Word of God and speaking what we want to see. This book will help you to consciously focus your thoughts on the truth of the scriptures, and speak faith words that will cause changes in your physical and spiritual atmosphere.

HONOUR FACTOR

Honour is the culture of God's kingdom! God is big on honour and so should we. It is His system of blessing and exalting His people. What then is honour? In this book, you will learn about honour — its principles, whom to honour, how to show honour God's way, the pitfalls of a lack of honour, and the benefits of honouring God, His people and His things.

THE REMNANT GENERATION

What time is it now? It is the time of great shaking that will reveal those who truly believe God and are ready to do His Word, His work, and His will in these end times — They are the Remnant! This book will show you God's method of preserving His Kingdom on earth and protecting His work and agenda for mankind.

Contact Information

Africa: +234 817 744 5013 **USA:** +1 346 580 7506
www.andrewosakweministries.org

www.ingramcontent.com/pod-product-compliance
Lightning Source LLC
Chambersburg PA
CBHW032209040426
42449CB00005B/508